Anywhere
But
NINEVEH!

Some books take much reading and leave little impression. This wonderful book takes little reading but leaves a deep impression. Daily portions of Jonah make for a rich diet – edifying, humbling and encouraging, with challenging insight and perceptive prayer. One cannot but fail to travel with Jonah into a deeper awareness of the purposes of God, ultimately to be found in the Lord Jesus Christ. This is a book rich in the grace that drives us to our knees and to the heart of our loving, forgiving, sovereign Lord.

SIMON AUSTEN
Rector, St Leonard's, Exeter, UK

Through a skilful re-telling of Jonah's story, this gem of a book has pastoral warmth, penetrating application, and a simplicity and directness that will challenge and inspire your walk with God. It exposes our fears, helps us to pray, points us to Christ, and refreshes our souls. Prayerfully read a section each day, and within the month your understanding of God and your motivation to serve Him will surely have changed!

JONATHAN LAMB
IFES Vice President
CEO and minister-at-large, Keswick Ministries

Anywhere
But
NINEVEH!

A month's Journey with Jonah

Frank Sellar

Frank Sellar is senior minister at Bloomfield Presbyterian Church in Belfast having served in Ireland, South and North for the last three decades. In June 2016 he was elected Moderator of the General Assembly of the Presbyterian Church in Ireland. Frank and Claire have three children, Rebecca (married to Christopher), Robert and Ruth.

Copyright © Frank Sellar 2016

paperback ISBN: 978-1-78191-862-3
epub ISBN: 978-1-78191-867-8
mobi ISBN: 978-1-78191-868-5

10 9 8 7 6 5 4 3 2 1

Published in 2016
by
Christian Focus Publications Ltd,
Geanies House, Fearn,
Ross-shire, IV20 1TW, Scotland.
www.christianfocus.com

Cover design by Daniel van Straaten

Printed by Nørhaven, Denmark

CONTENTS

Dedication

*In grateful appreciation of Dr Helen Roseveare:
selfless cross-cultural missionary, indefatigable
encourager and family friend.*

How to use this book

This is an attempt to introduce you to a person through a whole book of the Bible. Taking the text of Jonah verse by verse, and making observations on what it says, what it meant when originally written and what it means for us today, you are invited to study this Old Testament prophet day by day over the period of one month (31 days) and so to make it your own.

And the person I'd like you to meet is the one 'greater than Jonah': the Lord Jesus.

Introduction
JONAH

'Right Hand, Left Hand'

My ancestors were whalers from the north-east of Scotland. In the year 1852 Captain George Sellar from Peterhead, of the schooner *Agostina*, (to the horror of my youngest daughter) took 9,852 seals on an Arctic expedition. Factual though this may be, that's not however where my interest in Jonah and the whale came from! Rather it was as the result of an encounter with God some years ago. A speaker at our Christian Union at Queen's University in Belfast had spoken from Romans 12:11 *'Never flag in zeal. Be aglow with the Spirit. Serve the Lord'* (rsv) and his life personified these challenging words. That's how I, as a young believer in the Lord Jesus Christ, wanted to be! Shortly after, I was invited to serve on the staff of the Universities and Colleges Christian Fellowship (IFES) in the

Republic of Ireland. That may not seem of great consequence to many, but to me at that time it was. As a Northern Ireland Protestant from the unionist tradition, to be asked to live and work in a Southern Irish Catholic and republican context in the height of what were known as 'the troubles' seemed to me to be like Jonah the Israelite being summoned to preach in Nineveh. 'Oh Lord,' I said. 'Please No! I'm willing to go to Africa: Go to India: Do anything, Go anywhere, as long as it's not the Republic of Ireland.' Being a passionate believer in Jesus didn't preclude me from being a prejudiced bigot. And God replied to my plea as clearly as ever I've heard His voice: 'Frank, If you are not willing to serve in the South of Ireland I can't use you in Africa, India or anywhere else for that matter.'

Looking back, I'm not proud of that encounter. It embarrasses me, but I share it with you none the less in order to explain my specific affinity with Jonah - this complex and tangled-up servant. **Is God vindictive? Looking to see how He can make His servants as unhappy as they possibly could be?** Does God delight in making His people miserable? This then isn't merely a story about a prophet who lived some 2,800 years ago but is an intensely personal narrative which speaks directly into my soul and which you are invited to share too: *'Should I not be concerned about that great city where 120,000 people cannot tell their right hand from their left?'*

1

Jonah 1:1

God's Word

God speaks. That's the first thing that we read in this book of Jonah. The Lord is someone who does not hide or remain hidden but who communicates. Sometimes people say 'God is concealed' or 'I can't find Him' but the story of Jonah makes plain that it's not God who hides from us. It is Jonah who tries to hide from God! Ever since Adam and Eve hid themselves from the presence of the Lord in the Garden of Eden, humankind have sought to run away from having to listen to what God is saying but *'The Word of the Lord came to Jonah son of Amittai'*....

We don't know how this word came to Jonah, except that Jonah was someone not unfamiliar with hearing what God had got to say. He was a prophet who lived in Gath-Hepher, a town of Galilee during the first half of the eighth century B.C. around the same time as Amos and Hosea (2 Kings 14:25). Prophets first hear what God has got to say and then proclaim that word to others, and his role was to prophesy in the northern Kingdom of Israel during the reign of Jeroboam II. He would have been acquainted with other great prophets such as Elijah and Elisha who likewise had no difficulty hearing God speak. Was it with an audible voice or through a dream or visitation? Maybe verse 3 gives a hint when it says that 'Jonah fled from the presence of the Lord'. God had met with him in a special way, and as someone trained to discern the voice of God (2 Kings 2:3-8 and 4:38-44) he was able to tell the difference between an authentic message and the mere projection of his imagination. Certainly Jonah wouldn't have thought up this word of his own volition! Despite being a person who wanted to be a mouthpiece for the Living Lord, this was neither a message he wanted to hear nor to proclaim!

John's gospel tells us that God speaks clearly. God wants people to hear what He has got to say, and the supreme way in which God communicates is through His 'Word made human'. Eugene Peterson paraphrases John 1:14 in this way:-

The Word became flesh and blood and moved into the neighbourhood. We saw the glory with our our eyes, the one-of-a-kind glory, like Father, like Son, generous inside and out, true from start to finish'. (The Message)

God has not remained hidden. He has spoken to us through His Son the Lord Jesus. What is it that God has got to say through Him today that we, and others, need to hear?

Prayer: Heavenly Father, thank you that you are a communicating God who is far more keen to let us know your thoughts than we are to find them out. Please give us ears that are tuned in to your voice and hearts that are sensitive to your presence. May the Holy Spirit guide us as we discover your purposes through Jesus Christ, the Word made flesh. Amen.

2
JONAH 1:2
Great City 'Go'

God has no difficulty making Himself known. *'Go to the great city of Nineveh and preach against it, because its wickedness has come up before me.'*

It wasn't an easy command. Sometimes Christian people today fear that God will ask of them what He evidently demanded of Jonah. Ask them to do something really horrible. Force them to go to the worst possible place imaginable in order to make them utterly miserable!

Nineveh was the capital city of Israel's number one enemy – neighbouring state Assyria. 'Anywhere Lord but Nineveh!' There may have been at least three reasons why Nineveh was the last place on earth Jonah would have wanted to prophesy: It was a wicked place. No one wants to go to somewhere like Sodom either today or

Gomorrah! It was a foreign place. Jonah neither knew the culture nor liked it, and it was a hostile place. Today its ruins are found beside the River Tigris opposite Mosul in Iraq. Then, its great buildings spoke of arrogance, brutality and military prowess. Nineveh was notorious for its vicious torture and imperialist brazenness. But that's precisely why God wanted His prophet Jonah to go! Because it was wicked, that's why it needed to hear the gospel! As the Apostle Paul said years later to the church in another great city: *'How, then, can they call on the one they have not believed in? And how can they believe in the one of whom they have not heard? And how can they hear without someone preaching to them? And how can they preach unless they are sent?'* (Rom. 10:14) God could see that the wrong choices Nineveh was making were inevitably going to lead to trouble. But God wanted that great city to thrive, not dive!

Because it was a foreign place, the people would or could not 'come' to Zion: that's why Jonah needed to 'go' so that the people could hear the good news of flourishing!

In Acts 13:47 quoting the Old Testament prophet Isaiah, Paul and Barnabas said to their fellow Jews: *'This is what the Lord has commanded us: "I have made you a light for the Gentiles, that you may bring salvation to the ends of the earth!"'*

Because it was a hostile place that's why Jesus said *'It is not the healthy who need a doctor but the sick. I have not come to call the righteous, but sinners'* (Mark 2:17). Anyone can enjoy the company of those who are well. It requires the Holy Spirit's strength to minister to those who know they are not well!

And while Nineveh may indeed have been fearful, dangerous and hostile, God never asks His servants to do anything without also equipping them for the task. In Matthew 5 Jesus tells His followers precisely how to minister in places of extreme difficulty: *'You have heard it said, "Love your neighbour and hate your enemy." But I tell you: Love your enemies and pray for those who persecute you, that you may be sons of your Father in Heaven'* (vv. 43-44).

God doesn't ask His disciples to do the things they least desire to do. God loves to change His people's hearts so that they are happy to do the thing God wants them to do!

Prayer: Heavenly Father, great cities and nations of this world are in deep trouble. They need people who will be obedient to your call and, in spite of anxiety, prejudice or a sense of inadequacy, to 'Go'. Please change me so that I may discover that my deepest delight is in your service. Amen.

3

Jonah 1:3

But Jonah went down

'But Jonah ran away from the LORD and headed for Tarshish. He went down to Joppa, where he found a ship bound for that port. After paying the fare, he went aboard and sailed for Tarshish to flee from the LORD.'

Why did Jonah not want to go? He experienced something about God he wished was not true and so, instead of wanting God to change his attitude toward the foreigners of the Great city of Nineveh, Jonah preferred to trust himself to Gentile sailors and get on board a ship to sail across the Great Sea! Jewish people didn't like the sea. To them it was a place of chaos and crisis, terror and turmoil. Jesus in Mark 4:35-41 'calmed the sea' and with it soothed His troubled disciples. In heaven, Revelation 21 tells us that there will be no more sea, for the new creation brought about by Christ's redemption will be a place of total calmness and contentment, happiness and peace.

Sally Lloyd-Jones in her *Jesus Storybook Bible* writes, 'Jonah went ahead with his not-very-good plan. "One ticket to NOT Nineveh, please!" he said, and boarded a boat sailing in the very opposite direction of Nineveh.' It wasn't a very good idea because Jonah must have been aware of Psalm 139 which says: *'Where can I go from your Spirit? Where can I flee from your presence? If I go up to the heavens, you are there: if I make my bed in the depths, you are there. If I rise on the wings of the dawn, if I settle on the far side of the sea, even there your hand will guide me, your right hand will hold me fast'* (vv. 7-10). But so determined was Jonah to get away that maybe he even rejoiced in the providence of a boat being made ready at the port to take him away to the furthest place known in the ancient world! 'Out of sight and out of mind? Perhaps God will now find somebody else to do His dirty work instead?' Here is a prophet who is the total opposite of a disciple ready to 'Go' into all the world!

When believing people run away from the Lord, it is a downward spiral. The text tells us '[Jonah] went down to Joppa'. Soon he would go further 'down into the ship' below deck and later 'down into the depths of the sea'. But God doesn't want us to 'go down'! He wants us to 'rise up'! We have been made to glorify God and to enjoy Him forever. True happiness is found living in partnership with God rather than resisting Him. *'You have made known to me the path of life, you will fill me with joy in your presence, with eternal pleasures at your right hand.'* (Ps. 16:11)

Prayer: Heavenly Father, It's impossible to flee from your omnipresence but it's easy to run away from your felt presence. Create within me such disquiet when I am out of step with the Holy Spirit that I immediately want to return back to you, rather than going on a damaging downward spiral.

In Jesus' name I pray. Amen

4 JONAH 1:4

Great Wind

'Then the LORD sent a great wind on the sea, and such a violent storm arose that the ship threatened to break up.'

If Jonah thought he could enjoy a Mediterranean Cruise when he ought to have been in the Lord's service, he was in for a shock! God who in Jonah's own words (v. 9) *made* the sea and the land would use all kinds of natural phenomena to bring Jonah back to his senses: the wind, a storm, a fish, vomit, a plant, a worm and the scorching sun. If Jonah refused to go to that Great City, God would send a Great Wind to blow upon the Great Sea in order to make a Great impression upon the recalcitrant prophet!

Jonah wasn't the only prophet ever to be caught in a storm on the Mediterranean. Eight centuries later the circumstances though could not have been more different. The Apostle Paul was not fleeing from the presence of the Lord but was being transported to Rome out of obedience to the Lord (Acts 27:13-44). Paul stood up in front of the sailors and said *'Now I urge you to keep up your courage, because not one of you will be lost ... . Last night an angel of the God whose I am and whom I serve stood beside me and said, "Do not be afraid, Paul. You must stand trial before Caesar; and God has graciously given you the lives of all who sail with you." So keep up your courage, men!'* (vv. 22-25a).

It is perfectly possible for the Lord, the maker of Heaven and Earth, to use natural elements either to warn us or to encourage us; but either way it is in order to further His purposes of grace in our and others' lives and to give opportunity to rely more fully upon Him. Whether we are running away from God or seeking to be obedient to Him, it is wise to ask what God might be saying through events in the natural world and circumstances of life. It was the Lord after all who sent the Great Wind on the Great Sea in order to achieve His Great purposes of Grace.

Prayer: Heavenly Father, your word tells me that you chasten those you love. Grant me wisdom to interpret what you are saying through the natural events of life and may these be opportunities to discern your sovereign hand in my circumstances, in order that I may live obediently and serve lavishly. For Jesus' sake. Amen

5
Jonah 1:5
But Jonah

'All the sailors were afraid and each cried out to his own god. And they threw the cargo into the sea to lighten the ship. But Jonah had gone below deck, where he lay down and fell into a deep sleep.'

It's interesting how the unexpected or challenging circumstances of life can serve as a moment of reflection and reprioritisation. Suddenly the cargo that had seemed so valuable in port became a heavy and cumbersome burden at sea and the best thing to do was to get rid of it. The valuable collection of ornaments on the mantlepiece seem so worthless when their owner lies dying in a hospital bed. In the middle of the storm the sailors were terrified and cried out to their own god. 'There are no atheists in foxholes' famously contended someone who participated in the fierce conflict which was the Battle of Bataan in January 1942 when Japanese

Imperial forces gained victory over Americans in the Philippines. Cornell University examined 949 post-combat infantrymen and observed that these soldiers' reliance on prayer rose from 32 to 74 per cent as the battle intensified.

The ethnic mix of sailors on board meant that each cried out to the deity of their specific community in the hope that their particular patron might in turn make request to their divine superiors, eventually bringing the need before the god responsible for this calamitous storm.

'But Jonah'…there's that phrase again…was so unconcerned about others that prayer to his God was the last thing on his radar. He was asleep!

In the face of difficulties, traumas and desperate needs which our society and the world encounters: where are the people who believe in 'The Lord, the God of heaven, who made the sea and dry land'? While others cry out in vain to gods that are no gods, are those who know the Living God fast asleep? Blissfully unconcerned while multitudes of people perish?

Prayer: 'Where other lords beside Thee hold their unhindered sway, Where forces that defied Thee defy Thee still today. With none to heed their crying, for life and love and light, Unnumbered souls are dying and pass into the night'. Heavenly Father, shake us from our lethargy and grant us the heart and spirit of Christ we pray. Amen.

6 Jonah 1:6

Get up!

When was the last time someone told you to 'get up'? Chances are it was when you were a teenager. 'Get up,' said the exasperated ship's captain to the childish Jonah running away from God. 'How can you sleep when everybody else is working so hard?' 'How can you remain in your bunk while everybody else is crying out to their deities and you are not!' *'Get up and call on your god! Maybe he will take notice of us, and we will not perish!'* This speaks volumes about Jonah's frame of mind at this time. Deep in the belly of the ship Jonah was so unthinking it took a pagan sea captain to wake Jonah out of his lethargy: a polytheistic sailor had to tell an Israelite prophet he ought to be praying! The truth is, Jonah had chosen to suppress his conscience. He had silenced it. The storms and the angry wind and waves had failed to remind

29

him of his guilt, but now echoes of Jonah's original call by God in verse 2 to 'Arise and go!' are heard from the mouth of the ship's captain: 'Arise and pray!' There can be numerous reasons why, like Jonah, we do not pray. We might be too tired! We might not want to be in communication with God because we think we know what He will ask of us! We might think 'my prayers won't make any difference anyway. Sure there are plenty of other people who can do the praying for me!' A backsliding student from Ireland was once on a school trip to Kenya where he was doing humanitarian work in one of the townships. There he met some people in dire need and one of them suddenly turned to him and said, 'Pray for me!' Whatever the effect of his stuttering words in that situation, this stranger's request was the wake-up call this teenager needed to stop avoiding God and start being obedient.

Prayer: Heavenly Father, sometimes you use the most unlikely people and the strangest events to bring us to our senses; to stop resisting you and start appreciating the privilege it is to pray in the name of Jesus. Thank you for such prompts in my life and may I not become resistant to their impact, for Christ's glory. Amen

7

JONAH 1:7

Lots cast

'Then the sailors said to each other, "Come, let us cast lots to find out who is responsible for this calamity." They cast lots and the lot fell on Jonah.'

Surprise, surprise! The lot fell on Jonah! If God could use a pagan sailor to prompt the prophet to pray, it's no shock to see God using a game of chance to further reveal His will! The land of Canaan after all had been divided among the Israelites by lot and the duties of each tribe for Temple service were assigned likewise. Christian people do not have to resort to 'heads or tails' in order to determine the divine will. God has given His Holy Spirit to dwell within our hearts and His Word, the Scriptures of the Old and New Testaments, to incline our minds toward His will (John 16:12-15). Christians are not in the same position as these sailors who had neither the Spirit nor the Bible to guide them. But in this situation it was not by 'chance' that Jonah was identified as the one responsible for this trouble. In Numbers 32:23 Moses reminds the people that *You may be sure that your sin will find you out*. In Luke 12:2 Jesus put it this way: *There is nothing concealed that will not be disclosed, or hidden that will not be made known. What you have said in the dark will be heard in the daylight, and what you have whispered in the inner rooms will be proclaimed from the roofs*. Even as Jonah was found out by pagan sailors by lot, so it is impossible to avoid the gaze of God who sees all things, for as the proverb says, *The eyes of the Lord are everywhere, keeping watch on the wicked and the good*' (Prov. 15:3). It must have been extremely discomforting to Jonah to be found out. *If I say, "Surely the darkness will hide me and the light become night around me," even the darkness will not be dark to you; the night will shine like the day, for darkness is as light to you*' (Ps. 139:11-12). This however is not meant to be a threat! For the believer wanting to be in the centre of God's will, it is a wonderful, reassuring promise.

Prayer: Heavenly Father, thank you that neither death nor life, neither the present nor the future, neither height nor depth, nor anything else in all creation can separate us from the love of God that is in Christ Jesus our Lord. May I not presume on your kindness, but only want to be in the centre of your good purposes, for Jesus' sake. Amen

8

JONAH 1:8

Questions, questions

Having discovered that Jonah was to blame, the sailors asked him, *'Tell us, who responsible for is making all this trouble for us? What do you do? Where do you come from? What is your country? From what people are you?'* These were unwelcome questions. Until this point Jonah had been happy to hide his *yarmulke* under his hooded storm jacket, but now he faced a torrent of questions. Up to now, Jonah had wanted to conceal his identity. He didn't wish anyone to know anything about him. He seemed ashamed of his heritage. But the sailors were not to be deflected. They wanted to find out any possible connections Jonah might have in order to make sense of the tempest.

A student from a missionary family started his university career wanting to do just like Jonah: to keep his head down as a believer. Having been known as a 'pastor's kid' all his life, now he just wanted to be anonymous for a change and start off college life fitting in with everybody else. But the truth was this: he wasn't just like everybody else, and on the very first evening while downing pints in the students' union, the other students demanded to know who he was, why he was there and what he thought about the meaning of life! It was pagan unbelievers who irritatingly got him to confess with his lips what he believed in his heart! (Rom. 10:9)

In 1 Peter 3:15 it says, *'In your hearts set apart Christ as Lord. Always be prepared to give an answer to everyone who asks you to give a reason for the hope that you have. But do this with gentleness'.* This is the opposite of what Jonah hoped! Jonah hadn't set apart the Living Lord in his disobedient spirit and the questions he was asked were like unwelcome intrusions. By contrast, the Christian can pray that even in a context of hostility, the Holy Spirit will go ahead of them preparing unbelievers to ask questions which will allow them to make positive responses. There's nothing more thrilling for a willing believer than to see God answering that prayer – at social events – who we chat to, on the bus – who we sit beside, out for a walk – 'Tell me: what do you do? Where do you come from? Don't you go to church?'…and the rest is a gift.

Prayer: Heavenly Father, instead of fearing questions, please will you help me to look forward to the questions that people might ask me today which could give opportunity to speak winsomely of you and grant me reliance upon your Holy Spirit. For Jesus' sake. Amen.

9 JONAH 1:9

Jonah's testimony

It can't have been his moment of choice to share 'This is my life', but even in his disobedience Jonah did a pretty good job in response to all those probing questions. He answered, *'I am a Hebrew and I worship the LORD; the God of heaven, who made the sea and the land'*. He identified himself as one of God's chosen people. He confessed that he was an active worshipper (not merely a passive observer) of YaHWeH the one and true God of heaven. And as if that were not enough he went on to acknowledge that his God was the maker of both the sea and the dry land. In other words, Jonah was confessing that he knew the actual storm on the sea that was causing them all this turmoil was because he was running away from the one who had made it and controlled it! Sometimes we can be called upon to share our testimony even when we don't want to. Sometimes we can be pushed to tell people about our faith even when it's not the moment of our choosing. Best though that we confess to whom we belong out of obedience rather than from a position of non-compliance.

There was however one question Jonah didn't answer in his reply. He provided no response to the sailors' enquiry, *'What do you do'*? At one time he would have been able to say, '*I am a prophet of the Living Lord*'. We know from 2 Kings 14:25 that he had been used by God in the past - but now? Instead of speaking on behalf of God to the people, he had nothing to say! He had no word from the Lord to give! Compare Jonah on the high seas in the middle of a vicious storm with the Apostle Paul in Acts 27:33-36. Standing on deck Paul was also able to testify to the LORD. ' *"For the last fourteen days you have been in constant suspense and have gone without food. ... Now I urge you to take some food. ... Not one of you will lose a single hair from his head".* *After this he took some bread and gave thanks to God in front of them all. ... They were all encouraged and ate'.*

Jonah's testimony led to the sailors' increased terror! Paul's testimony led to the sailors' increased encouragement!

Prayer: Heavenly Father, we recognise that when we pray to you we come to no localised deity but to The LORD, the maker of heaven and earth. Grant us opportunities to share what we have come to know of your greatness, power and mercy to us with those who have no such hope, for Jesus' sake. Amen

10

JONAH 1:10-12

More questions, an answer?

Jonah's testimony terrified the sailors and they asked, *'What have you done? (They knew he was running away from the LORD, because he had already told them so.) The sea was getting rougher and rougher. So they asked him, "What should we do to you to make the sea calm down for us?"'* As a fare-paying passenger perhaps the sailors expected Jonah to request them to take him back to Joppa? Maybe they anticipated him suggesting that they should all earnestly pray to Jonah's ocean-controlling God? Not so. *'"Pick me up and throw me into the sea," he replied, "and it will become calm. I know that it is my fault that this great storm has come upon you."'* There was no reason for everyone to perish just because of one man's sin. Jonah knew it, and so, despairing of being of any further use to God or in His service, there was only one thing for it. For him as the guilty man to die. How amazing to fast forward then to the one 'greater than Jonah' when an innocent man died for a multitude of peoples' wrongs! In order to bring about peace with God, the Lord Jesus out of a deep desire for the rescue of others, gave up His life for the salvation of many (Matt. 20:28). This is grace beyond measure. In Romans 5:6-8 Paul tells us, *'At just the right time, when we were still powerless, Christ died for the ungodly. Very rarely will anyone die for a righteous man, though for a good man someone might possibly dare to die. But God demonstrates his own love for us in this: While we were still sinners, Christ died for us'.*

Prayer:-

'Grace unmeasured, vast and free
That knew me from eternity
That called me out before my birth
To bring You glory on this earth
Grace amazing, pure and deep
That saw me in my misery
That took my curse and owned my blame
So I could bear Your righteous name'. (Getty)

Heavenly Father, thank you for the Lord Jesus who though innocent died for the guilty.

As Jesus gave up His life for me, enable me to respond with wholehearted surrender, enormous gratitude and deep-seated joy, for His name's sake. Amen.

11

Jonah 1:13-14

Pagan generosity

How it must have pained the heart of God that His chosen servant had become so turned in on himself that he no longer saw the need to reach other nations of the world. It must still grieve Him when those who have themselves received the revelation of God's salvation refuse to set foot in alien territory to share His message of judgment and mercy. Yet here, ironically the Gentile sailors were far more concerned to save the believing Jonah than Jonah was to save those who did not know the living God! *'Instead, the men did their best to row back to land. But they could not, for the sea grew even wilder than before.'* Is it more shocking that unbelievers can be as kind and good as these sailors, or that a believer such as Jonah can be as uncaring about the fate of others' physical and eternal destiny? The truth is many non-Christians display beautiful attributes of common humanity and many Christians display ugly residues of the unregenerate nature. Pagans' goodness is not enough to get them to heaven (why otherwise would Christ have had to die as an atonement for sin?) and believers' selfishness is not enough to keep them out (since salvation is by grace and not by works). But from those who have received much, much will be required (Luke 12:48) and believers have been chosen in Christ in order to be holy and blameless in His sight (Eph. 1:4). This gradual process of becoming Christ-like is the work of the Holy Spirit in the life-long process known as sanctification. (John 17:15-17)

But even more ironically, the believing prophet who had fled from God, not wishing to bring the message of salvation to Gentiles in Nineveh, ends up successfully bringing the gospel to Gentiles on board ship!

Prayer: Heavenly Father, thank you so much for the kindness and goodness displayed by so many people who profess no faith in you. May I never become satisfied with my own self-centredness but enable me as one within whom your Spirit dwells to want to become holy and compliant like Jesus, for His name's sake. Amen.

12

Jonah 1:15-16

Calm and terror

'Then they took Jonah and threw him overboard, and the raging sea grew calm. At this the men greatly feared the LORD, and they offered a sacrifice to the LORD and made vows to him'.

With all other alternatives gone, the sailors were left with little option other than do as Jonah had suggested. No sooner had Jonah plunged into the tumultuous surf but the sea became calmed and the sailors became greatly troubled! What a reversal. The sea was stilled but the seafarers were in turmoil! In Mark 4:35-41 something not dissimilar took place. Jesus and His disciples were crossing the Sea of Galilee. A furious squall came up and the waves broke over the boat so that it was nearly swamped. Jesus was asleep. *'Don't you care if we drown?'* shouted the distraught seamen. Jesus rebuked the wind and said to the waves, *'Quiet! Be still!'*

and all became quiet. And the disciples...they were terrified and asked, *'Who is this? Even the wind and waves obey him!'* The same God as in the book of Jonah, exercised control of the elements, and those who witnessed it were filled with holy fear.

Fear of the Lord is very different from fear of the things the Lord has made. It's one thing to be afraid of the elements. It's another thing to be in awe of God who fashioned the elements. Fear of created things can lead to turmoil of heart, but fear of the Lord can lead to transformation of life. Around the same time as Jonah, Isaiah the prophet had an encounter with the Lord which left him almost paralysed with fear: *'Woe is me! ... I am ruined! For I am a man of unclean lips, and I live among a people of unclean lips, and my eyes have seen the King, the LORD Almighty'*. Then one of the seraphs touched Isaiah's mouth with a live coal from the altar and said, *'See, this has touched your lips: your guilt is taken away and your sin atoned for'*. (Isa. 6:5-7) Meeting God is an awesome thing and involves atonement, sacrifice and response. That was the experience of Isaiah and that was the experience of these sailors too. Scarcely able to believe their eyes, they greatly feared the Lord and offered a sacrifice to Him out of sheer gratitude and praise to Jonah's God! As people who have benefited from the sacrificial atonement of the Lord Jesus, can we do any less than fear Him with holy awe?

'Fear Him, ye saints, and you will then have nothing else to fear;

Make you his service your delight; your wants shall be his care'.

Prayer:-Heavenly Father, How often I am afraid of things and of people which can do no more than harm the body. Grant me a godly awe of you, the living Lord of my soul, so that nothing else may be my concern but your glory, for Jesus' sake. Amen.

13

But the Lord

'But the LORD provided a great fish to swallow Jonah, and Jonah was inside the fish three days and three nights.'

It was the late Jim Philip, I think, who said, 'The whale is in-fact a red herring!' And so it is. There is no whale mentioned here. It's a great fish, and far from the fish being the most important part of this book, it only features in three verses, whereas the Great God concerned for the Great City features from start to finish! How easy it is to get distracted by the means God uses to fulfil His purposes rather than God Himself!

While the sailors fretted about what they were having to do with Jonah and while Jonah plunged into what he was certain would be his watery grave, the Lord provided a great fish to carry out His purposes of grace for Jonah. Have you ever felt you had got yourself into

45

a place of trouble out of which there was no escape? 'But the Lord provided!' Ever plunged so deep into misery that you thought there was no way out? 'But the Lord provided!' It may have taken a while of course. For Jonah he had a period of time to stop, to think and to reflect. Three is often used in scripture as a motif of completeness or finality and so for three days and three nights Jonah had the perfect length of time to think about the Lord's plan for his life which he had tried to escape.

Sometimes God's provision is astonishing! He provided safe passage through the Red Sea for the Children of Israel pursued by the Egyptians. He provided manna from heaven for them to eat in the desert and He provided bread for Elijah via ravens. And for sinners, God made the most astonishing, least expected provision of all time – His Son the Lord Jesus, nailed to a cruel cross and buried within the tomb for three days. *'If God is for us, who can be against us? He who did not spare his own Son, but gave him up for us all – how will he not also, along with him, graciously give us all things?'* (Rom. 8:31b-32).

Prayer: Heavenly Father, Thank you for your amazing provision for us in Jesus. Thank you that you provide in this most astonishing of ways! As Jesus died for us and was raised, may we too die with Him and be raised to a life of service and eternal joy, for His name's sake. Amen.

14 JONAH 2:1-2
Jonah's Prayer

'From inside the fish Jonah prayed to the LORD his God. He said: "In my distress I called to the LORD, and he answered me. From the depths of the grave I called for help and you listened to my cry".' As Alistair Begg has observed, 'The belly of the fish wasn't a great place for Jonah to live, but it was a great place for him to learn', and now Jonah cries out to the God he has been trying to avoid! After he has left God out of the picture and unlike the pagan sailors refused to pray on the ship, God now comes back into his thinking and Jonah prays! Verse two is like a summary of the whole prayer. It's a prayer shaped by the Psalms so familiar to the prophet and it's a prayer unconcerned by the 'correct' way to pray:

' "The proper way for a man to pray,"
Said Deacon Lemuel Keyes,

"And the only proper attitude,
 Is down upon his knees."

"No, I should say the way to pray,"
Said Reverend Doctor Wise,
"Is standing straight, with outstretched arms,
And rapt and upturned eyes."

"Oh no; no, no," said Elder Slow,
 "Such posture is too proud:
A man should pray with eyes fast closed
And head contritely bowed."

"It seems to me his hands should be
Austerely clasped in front,
With both thumbs pointing toward the
ground,"
Said Reverend Doctor Blunt.

"Las' year I fell in Hodgkin's well
Head first," said Cyrus Brown,
"With both my heels a-stickin' up,
My head a-p'inting down;

"An' I made a prayer right then an' there—
Best prayer I ever said,
The prayingest prayer I ever prayed,
A-standing on my head."'

The Prayer of Cyrus Brown By Sam Walter
Foss (1858–1911)

'Lord save me. Rescue me from all my fears'.

Prayer: Heavenly Father, Prevent me from thinking there is only one appropriate place for me to pray and only one correct posture. Thank you for this heart-felt prayer of Jonah reminding me that even having been hard of heart, I can come to you at any moment and in any circumstance and you listen and answer my cry. Amen.

15

Jonah 2:3-6

Sank down!

In distress for himself (in contrast to his lack of distress for the troubled sailors) Jonah implores for himself the mercy he would deny others, but in doing so he recognises that his descent into the deep is not merely a physical separation. It is a spiritual estrangement caused by his own disobedience, brought about by the sailors' actions but ultimately under the sovereign will of God: *'You hurled me into the deep, into the very heart of the seas, and the currents swirled about me; all your waves and breakers swept over me.'* God's great purpose was that the people of Nineveh might know salvation but Jonah didn't want that. Now in His providence God permits Jonah to experience what it is like to be out of fellowship with the Lord so that perhaps through this distress he might now empathise with the Ninevites in their need of rescuing. Sometimes when people have experienced something dreadful they describe it as 'hell', but terrifying though it may have been, no physical experience can ever come even close to the terror of eternal separation. Heaven is where God is found. Hell is the absence of God for ever. **I said, *'I have been banished from your sight.'*** Here was the believing Jonah out of communion with the Lord, ***'Yet I will look again towards your holy temple.'*** Even in the depths of the belly of the fish Jonah was able to discover the truth of what his fellow prophet wrote in Jeremiah 29:13, *'You will seek me and find me when you seek me with all your heart. I will be found by you'.* God had not given up on Jonah and he hasn't given up on you either! Whatever the depths to which you have sunk, God seeks to rescue and to restore! ***The engulfing waters threatened me, the deep surrounded me; seaweed was wrapped around my head. To the roots of the mountains I sank down; the earth beneath barred me in for ever. But you brought my life up from the pit, O LORD my God.'*** In a prayer infused with at least ten references to the Psalms, Jonah recalled these incredible scripture truths which had been part of his earlier life and now surfaced when he found himself wallowing in deep turmoil.

Prayer: Heavenly Father, whatever state I am in, whatever condition or dire straits I have got into, I turn to you. Not because I'm worthy, because I'm not, but because you are good and have promised to respond to those who seek you: I do not want to sink down any deeper. Please have mercy on me, Lord, and enable me to worship you again in spirit and in truth for Jesus' sake. Amen.

16

Jonah 2:7-10

Rise up!

Jonah sank down. God wanted to raise Jonah up. Sometimes people have to sink very far down before there is a turning to God for help.

'When my life was ebbing away, I remembered you, LORD, and my prayer rose to you, to your holy temple.'

Jonah 'remembered' the Lord, and the prophet who slept rather than prayed in the belly of the ship now was awake and prayed in the belly of the fish. He had sunk down as low as he could go, but now Jonah's prayer 'rose up' to the Lord. And this was his prayer:

'Those who cling to worthless idols forfeit the grace that could be theirs. But I, with a song of thanksgiving, will sacrifice to you. What I have vowed I will make good. Salvation comes from the LORD.'

This was an orthodox, insightful, eloquent prayer. Giving homage to idols is worthless because idols can never deliver. An idol is something people look to for things that only God can give. God's unmerited grace however is available to all who turn to the One True Living Lord in repentance and faith. Salvation is to be found in no person, place or thing other than the LORD. Neither the polytheistic idol-worshipping sailors nor the pagan syncretistic idol-loving Ninevites could find rescue in their worthless objects of worship, for as Peter proclaimed to the Sanhedrin some centuries later about Jesus of Nazareth, *'Salvation is found in no one else, for there is no other name given to mankind by which we must be saved'* (Acts 4:12). Jonah was right. What Jonah said was correct. **'Salvation comes from the LORD'!** The only thing was, Jonah's orthodox, insightful and eloquent words did not match the reality of his personal condition. Before Jonah could confront the people of Nineveh with their idols and proclaim the salvation that is to be found in the Lord alone, Jonah had to confront the idols of his own heart and surrender those to God.

It was much easier for Jonah to see the idols in other peoples' lives. Much more difficult to identify those things that preoccupied his own affections and prevented him from total surrender to the Lord: ethnicity, creed, culture. As Timothy Keller put it in 'Counterfeit Gods',

> 'His fear of personal failure, his pride in his religion, and his fierce love of his country had coalesced into a deadly idolatrous compound that spiritually blinded him to the grace of God. As a result he did not want to extend that grace to an entire city that needed it. He wanted to see them all dead.'

Was God sick of Jonah's myopia? *'And the Lord commanded the fish, and it vomited Jonah on to dry land'.*

Prayer: 'O for a closer walk with God, a calm and heavenly frame. A light to shine upon the road that leads me to the Lamb. ... The dearest idol I have known, whate'er that idol be, help me to tear it from Thy throne and worship only Thee.' Grant me an attitude of true repentance, for Jesus' sake, Amen. (William Cowper)

17

Jonah 3:1-2

God's Word (again)

Jonah must preach so that Nineveh, however godless and unbelieving, may still be the recipients of God's undeserved mercy. Having himself been the beneficiary of God's grace and clemency in the belly of the fish and pledged his loyalty to Him in a most profound way, now Jonah will surely be compliant and obedient? *'Then the word of the LORD came to Jonah a second time. Go to the great city of Nineveh and proclaim to it the message I give you.'* Granting him another chance, God was now calling Jonah on this second occasion. God's word does not change even if we ignore it. Its message does not alter even though we may not like to obey it. James Hudson Taylor said, 'The Great Commission is not an option to be considered: it is a command to be obeyed,' and so again God said, 'Go'. 'Go to the great city of Nineveh'. Not Tarshish. Not Jerusalem but Nineveh. 'Great' because of its architecture? Yes. 'Great' because of its intellectual and cultural reputation? Yes. 'Great' because of its huge need of the message *Jonah* would preach? Well, no! Jonah wasn't to proclaim his own message! He was to proclaim the message God would give him to preach! That after all is the prophet's role. He's not to give his own ideas. He's not to present his own opinions. He is to proclaim the message God gives him to say. That realisation is both daunting and liberating. Daunting because God's message may not be what we want to say. Liberating because it takes the pressure off the proclaimer to think up something to communicate! Daunting because the preacher must first be tuned in to God's wave-length and willing to be the human channel through whom God may speak. Liberating because there is a freedom in being the Lord's mouthpiece and knowing that God's word never returns to Him empty but accomplishes what He desires and achieves the purpose for which it is sent (Isa. 55:11). Jesus was the master communicator of God's word. When the people heard Him they knew He spoke as from God Himself. It was a compelling message. It was a message of freedom to which people were invited to respond and it was a message that so infuriated those in authority that they crucified Him.

Having once run away from the Lord's calling to proclaim His word, will Jonah now extend the same forbearance to Nineveh he experienced himself?

Prayer: Heavenly Father, having first received mercy through Jesus' death for me on the cross and benefited from second chances myself, grant me willingness to speak to others – not in my own wisdom but under your guidance, for Jesus' sake. Amen

18

JONAH 3:3

Obedience

'Jonah obeyed the word of the LORD and went to Nineveh. Now Nineveh was a very important city – a visit required three days.'

A change had indeed come about in Jonah's life (however reluctant), prefiguring the change which would come about in Nineveh's life. Jonah obeyed, and from the place where the fish had deposited him, he started out on the long and arduous journey of over 500 miles and probably at least a month. C.S. Lewis once observed, 'If you're on the wrong road, progress means doing an about-turn and walking back to the right road: in that case, the man who turns back soonest is the most progressive.' Jonah had lots to think about *en route*. Lots of time to consider God's character which is forbearing: *'The Lord is patient with you, not wanting anyone to perish, but everyone to come to repentance'* (2 Pet. 3:9). *'God our Saviour, who wants all men to be saved and to come to a knowledge of the truth'* (1 Tim. 2:4). He had plenty chance to pray and consider how best to navigate through the complex of streets that made up this great metropolis. Donald J. Wiseman has suggested that because Nineveh was such an important royal city, in keeping with ancient oriental practice of hospitality there may have been a three-day protocol whereby, on the first day you arrived, on the second day you went about the purpose of your visit and on the third day you prepared for return. Whatever, this was a city important to God and Jonah had a vital task on his arrival. Cities are hugely significant places. With nearly 38 million people, Tokyo tops the ranking of most populous megalopolises followed by Delhi, Shanghai, Mexico City, Sao Paulo and Mumbai. Cities are not just important because of their size but because of their legislative, judicial and cultural significance on the whole nation. Because cities have so many people there is greater opportunity for overt sinful practice than in the countryside, but also much more opportunity to reach people with the good news of salvation. Jeremiah urged his people in exile to seek the peace and prosperity of the city. *'Pray ... because if it prospers, you too will prosper'* (Jer. 29:7).

Prayer: Heavenly Father, thank you that you have a heart for the cities of this world. Grant me your heart of compassion for the welfare of all who govern, administer, service and maintain them and I pray for the church's life and witness among desperate human needs found in vast urban areas, for Jesus' glory. Amen.

19

JONAH 3:4-6

Forty Days

'On the first day, Jonah started into the city. He proclaimed: "Forty more days and Nineveh will be overturned." The Ninevites believed God. They declared a fast, and all of them, from the greatest to the least, put on sackcloth.'

No sooner had Jonah arrived in the great city than things began to happen! He hardly had time to unpack his rucksack and Jonah did what he had been asked to do: proclaim the message God required him to say, and the Ninevites believed God. It doesn't say they believed Jonah. They believed God. That's a sure sign the message had been faithfully delivered. The people weren't attracted by his lovely accent or by his oratorical skills. As Jonah spoke, the people heard God's voice and immediately responded. So convinced were they of the authenticity of the message that they repented. Whether these eight words were the sum total of what he proclaimed or a summary of the message, the effect upon the people was as dramatic as it was plain, from the most important citizens to the humblest of slaves. *'When the news reached the king of Nineveh, he rose from his throne, took off his royal robes, covered himself with sackcloth and sat down in the dust.'* The king along with his people repented. Ruler and ruled bowed to the authority of the spoken word. In Luke's Gospel 11:29-32, reacting to the people of His day questioning whether His miracles were done by the power of Beelzebub or God, Jesus said, *'This is a wicked generation. It asks for a miraculous sign, but none will be given it except the sign of Jonah. For as Jonah was a sign to the Ninevites, so also will the Son of Man be to this generation'.* Jonah's message was simple and clear and the people responded. Jesus also spoke with directness and clarity about His death and resurrection, but instead of responding like these pagan Gentiles, the religious people of Jesus' day reacted with disdain. As a result, *'The men of Nineveh will stand up at the judgment with this generation and condemn it; for they repented at the preaching of Jonah, and now one greater than Jonah is here'* (v. 32). Some rejected Jesus without even giving Him a proper hearing (John 7:50-51). Their spurning of Him, and through Him God's message of repentance, is grounds for serious regret. Failure to respond to the Son of Man who has spoken the word of God is cause for culpability.

Prayer: Heavenly Father, forgive me when I fail to listen to the sign of Jesus. Have mercy when I refuse to change my ways when I hear His message of faith and repentance and bring me to a renewed desire to live with a humble and contrite heart, for His name's sake. Amen.

20

JONAH 3:7-9

The King's decree

Then he issued a proclamation in Nineveh:

'By the decree of the King and his nobles: Do not let any man or beast, herd or flock, taste anything; do not let them eat or drink. But let man and beast be covered with sackcloth. Let everyone call urgently on God. Let them give up their evil ways and their violence. Who knows? God may yet relent and with compassion turn from his fierce anger so that we will not perish.'

Repentance was accompanied by signs. Under the King's leadership the people said 'sorry' not only with their lips but by their actions. Fervent prayer, fasting and outward illustration of their inner conviction was external evidence of their willingness to turn from their previous lifestyle and demonstrated their desire that God should spare them from destruction. Another prophet, (Joel 2:13-14) indicated that fasting and weeping and mourning were not enough in themselves. *'Rend your heart and not your garments. Return to the LORD your God, for he is gracious and compassionate, slow to anger and abounding in love, and he relents from sending calamity. Who knows? He may turn and have pity and leave behind a blessing'.* But how do we know if we have repented enough? This question has bothered many believers. Esau after all shed many tears but Jacob received his father's blessing. Judas wept bitterly but this was not the same as repentance. King David by contrast cast himself on the mercy of God and prayed, *'Against you, you only have I sinned and done what is evil in your sight.'* (Ps. 51:4) Having acknowledged his sin was against God and Him alone, he then relied on God to do for him what he could never do for himself: *'Create in me a pure heart, O God, and renew a steadfast spirit within me. Do not cast me from your presence or take your Holy Spirit from me. Restore to me the joy of your salvation and grant me a willing spirit, to sustain me'.* (Ps. 51:10-12) This was a pointer forward to Christ who entered in to our broken and rebellious humanity and lived a perfect life and died a perfect death so that we, who deserved nothing but separation from a holy God, might be restored and forgiven in Him.

We are not just healed by Christ but healed in and through Christ. He is the guarantor of our acceptance and the ground of our assurance.

Prayer: Heavenly Father, thank you for Jesus who experienced the flood of repentance for us in the Jordan river and a baptism of blood on the cross in Jerusalem. Enable us to enter into His life of repentance by His atoning death so that we who can do nothing to merit your favour, may experience everlasting life through Jesus Christ our Lord. Amen

21

JONAH 3:10

Compassion

When God saw what they did and how they turned from their evil ways, He had compassion and did not bring upon them the destruction He had threatened.

God had mercy on the Ninevites. As Martin Luther put it, 'The left hand of God's wrath is replaced by his right hand of blessing and freedom.' The Lord extended loving kindness to the people of that great city and refrained from punishment.

What a great place this would be for the book to end! Success, relief and everybody lived happily ever after. But irritatingly that's not where this story concludes! At the moment of Jonah's greatest triumph we gain an insight into his heart that both disconcerts and unnerves us. God is a God of grace. Jonah knew that from Psalm 103:8: *'The LORD is compassionate and gracious, slow to anger, abounding in love'*. God was like the loving father in Luke 15 who, on seeing his waster son while he was still a long way off, '*Filled with compassion for him, ran to his son, threw his arms around him and kissed him*'! Jonah knew that although his mission had been to 'preach against' the city for its wickedness there was always the possibility that judgment might indeed be averted!

If God was like the prodigal father and Nineveh was like the prodigal son, Jonah was like the elder brother in Jesus' parable. The older brother became angry and refused to go to the party. He was a self-righteous moralist. Unlike the worthless brother who had danced with prostitutes and eaten with pigs, Jonah had served the father all these years and now God 'owed him'!

But, says the Apostle Paul: 'God is God', and quoting Exodus 33:19, '*I will have mercy on whom I have mercy, and I will have compassion on whom I have compassion.*' (Rom. 9:15) Jonah had to learn to feel with God's heart and rejoice when sinners repent.

Prayer: Heavenly Father, if only life were straightforward and cut and dried. If only, during times of blessing, everything turned out well and all was straightforward. Lord, you still have a work of grace to perform in my heart right until the moment when you bring me into the new heaven and new earth. Thank you that you exercise mercy on religious people who are not yet sanctified as much as you do to previously irreligious people. Amen.

But Jonah was greatly displeased and became angry

God had compassion on the Ninevites and did not bring about the sort of overturning Jonah had anticipated, but instead of the messenger being delighted that the preaching had been heeded, such was the depth of his prejudice and racism, Jonah was upset and annoyed when the recipients of that message responded! The prophet who himself had benefited from God's mercy and salvation in the belly of the fish and liked it for himself, resented it when it was extended to those he felt were not deserving of God's forgiveness! Poor Jonah hadn't understood grace. 'God's riches at Christ's expense' isn't for nice people. God's mercy is not for 'worthy' saints but for unworthy sinners. The Apostle Paul (who we call a Saint) had the correct gospel insight. In 1 Timothy 1:15 he wrote: *'Christ Jesus came into the world to save sinners – of whom I am the worst. But for that very reason I was shown mercy so that in me, the worst of sinners, Christ Jesus might display his unlimited patience as an example for those who would believe on him and receive eternal life'.* The greatest hurdle for Jonah in discharging his missionary mandate was not the pagan sailors, nor the great fish, nor Nineveh's powerful ruler or ruthless people but Jonah himself! Jonah was angry because God was treating those outside the covenant with the same compassion as those within it. He was upset because God had shown mercy to a vicious and cruel imperial power that constantly threatened his homeland. Jonah felt Israel deserved better than for her God to show kindness to her enemies. The Jews were called to be light to the Gentiles but Jonah didn't want to shine the love of God's light to these 'dogs'. How easy to love God's grace when it is for 'me' but to resent it when extended to people 'not like me': to asylum seekers, to child-abusers, to Islamic Terrorists. It's only as we begin to appreciate the sheer depth of sin within our own hearts and the magnificence of God's mercy toward us, that took Jesus all the way to the cross, that we can begin to understand the Lord who wants to extend His mercy even to those we most fear.

Prayer: Heavenly Father, thank you for your mercy shown to me in the gospel. Forgive me when I am happy to keep that to myself instead of wanting to share it with others not like me. Change my heart so that I may develop your love of compassion even to people I dislike most, for Jesus' sake. Amen.

23

Gracious and Compassionate God

Jonah prayed to the Lord, *'O Lord, is this not what I said when I was still at home? That is why I was so quick to flee to Tarshish. I knew that you are a gracious and compassionate God, slow to anger and abounding in love, a God who relents from sending calamity. Now O Lord, take away my life, for it is better for me to die than to live'.*

It has been suggested that in Chapter One Jonah runs from God. In Chapter Two Jonah runs into God. In Chapter Three Jonah runs with God and in Chapter Four Jonah tries to run God! In this prayer Jonah was telling the Lord off. Jonah was saying to Almighty God, 'I knew this was going to happen!' It sounds so astonishing! Could it be that prayers we pray might also be every bit as absurd! Giving out to God and having the temerity to tell Him how

He ought to behave? Prayer can be a funny thing if we are the ones telling God what He really ought to do and what not to do. Having refused to pray on board ship and then having prayed a prayer of thanksgiving in the belly of the fish, now Jonah prays a really selfish, angry prayer. See how many times 'I','me' and 'my' appear in this outpouring? Six times. Less than perfect Jonah! O. Hallesby in his masterful book defines prayer as 'An offering up of our desires unto God, in the name of Christ, by the help of his Spirit; with confession of our sins, and thankful acknowledgement of his mercies.' William Still shares Brother Lawrence's conviction that prayer is practising the presence of God. 'Practically my every thought – about myself and about everyone else which comes to mind - should be shared with my ever-present Lord.' While Jonah does indeed pray here in Nineveh, it's not in order to develop a relationship of love and humility and trust but to scold! It's just as well the Lord is indeed gracious and compassionate, slow to anger and abounding in steadfast love! How good God is letting His children rant. But the Lord who is kind, merciful and forgiving wants Jonah to grow in grace and knowledge and love of Him and so He lets him speak before answering. How very different was Jonah compared to another preacher 'full of grace and truth' (John 1:14) who shed tears over the city to which he had come to preach: *'As Jesus approached Jerusalem and saw the city, he wept over it and said, "If you, even you, had only known on this day what would bring your peace...'* (Luke 19:41-42). *'O Jerusalem, ... how often I have longed to gather your children together, as a hen gathers her chicks under her wings, but you were not willing'* (Matt. 23:37).

Prayer: Heavenly Father, how very patient you are with us and with our prayers that are more often letting off steam and demanding things we want. Please align our hearts to yours so that even as Jesus prayed with tears, we too might have His compassion, not hardness of heart toward those in need of the Saviour. For His name's sake. Amen.

24

JONAH 4:4

But the Lord replied

Jonah prayed and God responded: *'Have you any right to be angry?'* Prayer is a two-way conversation and here we can see a fairly robust exchange! Jonah knew God to be slow to anger and yet Jonah is angry! Jonah questioned God for not being exasperated at the Ninevites and God questioned Jonah for being resentful with Him! Jonah's theology about God was correct but his personal prejudice against people he did not think God should like overshadowed what he knew to be the Lord's will. His understanding of Scripture and his heart were in conflict. His orthodoxy knew, *'It is by grace we are saved, through faith – and this not from yourselves, it is the gift of God – not by works, so that no-one can boast.'* (Eph. 2:8-9) But his heart said, 'I and my people are better than them. We deserve to be saved. They don't'! Chapter 4:1 said '*But Jonah*' and now Ch. 4:4 says '***But the LORD***'. It's good that in prayer we can be honest with God. We may as well be because as Psalm 139:4 reminds us, '*Before a word is on my tongue you know it completely, O LORD*'. But just because we are honest, does not mean to say that it is the final word: '*But the LORD*'! Thank God for '*But the LORD*'. God did not call Jonah to Nineveh because he was special. He called him because God had a message of hope and salvation to give through him to people who, without Him, were heading for self-destruction. And God will not permit His servants to wallow in the joy of their own salvation while at the same time wishing for the annihilation of others. This will not do! Unwarranted and out-of-proportion anger against God for His mercy and grace to people we do not like cannot remain unchallenged by the maker of heaven and earth. God confronted Jonah with the idols of his heart: pride in his religion, ethnicity and culture, which when contested led to irrational fury.

Prayer: Heavenly Father, forgive us that when our hopes and passions are dashed, we display sinful anger towards you and other people. Save us from the idolatry of making good things into ultimate things and help us find our meaning and fulfilment in you and in your glory alone. Amen.

25

Jonah 4:5

Silent treatment

Jonah didn't reply! God had responded to his prayer (v. 4) but Jonah didn't reply to God's answer! Instead he gave God 'the silent treatment'. *Jonah went out and sat down at a place east of the city. There he made himself a shelter, sat in its shade and waited to see what would happen to the city'.* Sometimes children think that if they hide their head under a pillow they can't be seen and sometimes adults think that if they ignore God then maybe He can't see them either! But giving God the silent treatment is no more effective than trying to run away to Tarshish. In his childishness Jonah took things into his own hands. He went outside the city walls and sat down. He made himself a hut and waited. If God didn't do what he wanted and if God didn't think the way he thought God ought to think, then there was only one thing to do… pout! The truth was this, God was not a Jewish nationalist but Jonah thought He should be. Yes, God was covenantally committed to Israel but that was not to the exclusion of everyone else. Jonah was proud of his nation and felt God ought to share this attitude too. Jonah loved his wee country but felt God ought to dislike the traditional enemy nation too. When personal bigotry and political prejudice are projected on to God, it's a grave mistake. The Apostle Paul had once been a Jewish nationalist. *'Circumcised on the eighth day, of the people of Israel, of the tribe of Benjamin, a Hebrew of Hebrews, … a Pharisee'* (Phil. 3:5), but God had helped him see that his Jewishness did not have to make him into a hard-hearted Xenophobe; for in Romans 9:15 Paul quotes Exodus 33:19 where the Lord says, *'I will have mercy on whom I have mercy, and I will have compassion on whom I have compassion'* and then came to say: *'I raised you up for this very purpose, that my name might be proclaimed in all the earth'* (Rom. 9:17). Jonah didn't like the answer God had given to him. You would now expect God to yell at this narrow-minded prejudiced man who had the temerity to give God the silent treatment, but in keeping with His character, the Lord is still as compassionate towards the bigoted Jonah as He had been towards his bitter enemy Nineveh!

Prayer: Heavenly Father, how easy it can be for us to imbibe the sinful prejudices of secular society into our own hearts and sometimes even to be more bigoted than unbelievers! Have mercy on us. Expose our racism and destroy fear by your grace so that we may be liberated to see people as gifts rather than as problems, through Christ our Lord. Amen

26

JONAH 4:6-8

Plant and worm, wind and sun

You would have thought that God would have got fed up with Jonah giving Him the silent treatment, and responded with a comment such as 'Where would you be today if I had treated you the same way you have treated Nineveh?' Instead we read the Lord 'provided' for Jonah! That's what a compassionate and generous God does! In the same way God provided a big fish to rescue Jonah from the deep sea, so now God provided other natural things for his benefit. *'Then the LORD God provided a vine and made it grow up over Jonah to give shade for his head to ease his discomfort, and Jonah was very happy about the vine. But at dawn the next day God provided a worm, which chewed the vine so that it withered.'* There has been some conjecture pertaining to the nature of this vine. Some have suggested it was in fact a caster oil plant to give Jonah a dose of his own medicine. What is of greater import is that the word translated here as 'discomfort' is the same word found in 3:10 where God did not bring about the 'calamity' or 'disaster' threatened on Nineveh. God was indeed giving Jonah an object lesson. Jonah was very happy with the plant and 'discomforted' when it withered. It was a 'disaster' to him when the plant died! *'When the sun rose, God provided a scorching east wind, and the sun blazed on Jonah's head so that he became faint. He wanted to die and said "It would be better for me to die than to live".'* Jonah's world ended for him when his comfort blanket was removed. This was not of course the only time Jonah had wanted to die. In the midst of the storm at 1:12 he had ordered the sailors to cast him into the sea, down into the depths of the grave. In his prayer in 4:3 he had expressed his wish to die rather than live. Depressed, upset, and suicidal, Jonah was not the first prophet to feel this way. Sitting under a broom tree (1 Kings 19:4) Elijah said to God, *'I have had enough, Lord! Take my life. I am no better than my ancestors'.* Sadly, self-harm thoughts are not beyond the experience of servants of God. The difference between Elijah and Jonah though was that Elijah had been obedient and zealous for the Lord God whereas Jonah had been disobedient and self-interested for himself. His egotism now merited a hard question to be put to him by the Lord.

Prayer: Heavenly Father, I pray today for any who, because of their service for you or even out of their own fault, have thoughts of suicide. Please will you minister to them according to their need and according to your great mercy and along with the Psalmist pray for them: *'Do not cast me from your presence or take your Holy Spirit from me. Restore to me the joy of your salvation and grant me a willing spirit to sustain me'.* (Ps. 51:11-12) Amen.

27

Jonah 4:9

But God

But God (again) **said to Jonah, 'Do you have a right to be angry about the vine?'** It's easy for human beings to be angry at God. 'How can a loving God let this bad thing happen to me?' (Or in this story, 'How can a loving God let this especially *good* thing happen to the Ninevites!') But what if God were to say to us, 'How could *you* let all these wicked things happen in this lovely world I entrusted to *your* stewardship and care?'

Thomas Carlisle wrote:-

> 'And Jonah stalked to his shaded seat
> and waited for God to come around to his way
>   of thinking.
> And God is still waiting for a host of Jonahs
> in their comfortable houses
> to come around to his way of loving.'

*'Do you have a right to be angry about the
      vine?'
'I do', he said. 'I am angry enough to die!'*

In the words of Eugene Peterson 'Jonah thought
he had come to Nineveh to do a religious job,
to administer a religious programme. God
had brought Jonah to Nineveh to give him
an experience of amazing grace'. The tables
are turned: it is no longer Jonah preaching to
the people of Nineveh but Jonah invited to
a vocation far beyond anything he had imagined.
Far from being humbled by this enquiry, Jonah
broke his silence to God's previous question in
verse 4 and responded sharply, *'Of course I have
a right to be angry'!*

How quick we are to defend our own rights,
slow to consider the prerogatives of others,
but God wanted Jonah not just to think but
to feel what it was like to stand in somebody
else's sandals for even a brief moment. God is
still interested in changing stubborn, slow to
change, irritable Jonahs into messengers of the
gospel, and if that requires giving a moment's
discomfort so that we begin to see things from
God's perspective rather than from our own,
He will do it. Jonah seemed to care more about
his vine than about the people that God wanted
to save. How absurd! We wouldn't be like that!
Would we? One day our youngest child was
playing in the garden. She accidentally knocked

off the head of a tulip. I loved that tulip because it was the first spring blossom in that flower-bed. It was beautiful. 'Look what you've done to my plant,' I railed. And do you know what I sensed God say to me? 'You get upset over this tulip and yet you don't get hot and bothered about the countless people suffering right now in the Middle East'.

Prayer: Heavenly Father, how fickle we are. What self-consumed creatures! Forgive us for valuing 'things' more than people. Have mercy on us for focusing our attention on trifles when the world is crying out for love, care and the hope of the gospel. Shake us out of our complacency and help us see the world as you see it, for Jesus' sake. Amen.

28

JONAH 4:10-11

But the Lord

The start of this story begins with God and that's where it ends too. He has both the first and the last word! The same Lord who said *'Go'* now said, *'You have been concerned about this vine, though you did not tend it or make it grow. It sprang up overnight and died overnight. But Nineveh has more than a hundred and twenty thousand people who cannot tell their right hand from their left, and many cattle as well. Should I not be concerned about that great city?'* You have been angry about the demise of a plant in which you had no emotional investment. Do I not have a right to feel as you feel about this vine for poor hapless people? Concerned as you were by the vine, should I not be concerned for this great city?

Moved by the large crowds who followed Him, Mark 6:34 tells us, *'[Jesus] had compassion on them because they were like sheep without a shepherd'*. The vulnerable people needed pastoral care and attention. They required protection from wild wolves. They were crying out for a Good Shepherd who would come to their aid. And that's precisely what Jesus did. The Good Shepherd became the sacrificial lamb for those in need of a Saviour. As foolish, straying sheep who have got trapped and are unable to free themselves, Jesus came to our rescue.

In addressing Jonah who seemed more concerned about the demise of his shelter than the spiritual condition of thousands of people, might he who was so anxious about plant life now at least be moved by the fate of cows?

The Ninevites' right-left discrimination difficulties had nothing to do with their intelligence or lack of it. It was a way of saying they were ordinary people who simply needed concern. God loves with equal compassion those who dig with their right or their left foot, and those unable to tell the difference between the two.

Prayer: Heavenly Father, you are concerned for the salvation and restoration of the whole of creation. In the Kingdom of your Son there will be a new heaven and new earth, Eden restored. As your people, called and filled with your Holy Spirit, enable us in turn to be concerned enough to go, to love, to proclaim and to care for this world you loved so much Christ died in order to save. Amen

29

Jonah 1:1

And us?

'The word of the LORD came to Jonah: "Go".'
As we saw at the start, God is a God who
communicates. The Lord is the Lord who
commands. The God who in the beginning
said, *'Let there be light'* and there was light spoke
and things happened (Gen. 1:3). The Lord who
called His disciples beside the Sea of Galilee and
said, *'Come, follow me'* - and at once they got
up and followed (Mark 1:17). God spoke to the
wind, and it blew! He spoke to the fish, and it
swallowed! He spoke to the fish, and it vomited!
He spoke to the plant, and it grew! He spoke
to the worm, and it chewed! He spoke to the
scorching east wind, and it blew! He spoke to
the sun, and it shone! And He spoke to Jonah
and Jonah said 'NO'! Every creature animate
and inanimate obeyed, except a self-consumed
reluctant (believing!) human being!

But God is God and Jonah is not and Jonah discovered that while it pained the heart of the Lord to be spurned, God did not, and God would not, give up on His defiant servant!

Surely the heart of humankind is rebellious. God had every right to destroy Jonah and those creatures that defy His word, but the gospel is that *'The Lord is a gracious and compassionate God, slow to anger and abounding in steadfast love'* and in His mercy and grace God Himself provided His Son as a perfect sacrifice who would offer Himself; the innocent for the guilty, the perfect obedient one for disobedient headstrong creatures such as us. On the Cross, Jesus bore the penalty for our rebellion, so that we who deserved nothing but death and banishment for ever in the depths of Sheol, might instead receive forgiveness and grace.

There are two ways of experiencing God. One is the hard way. It's the way of running away from Him. Setting our face against His purpose and failing to enjoy God. The other is also the hard way! It is the way of obedience. Jesus never promised being His disciple would be easy. *'Take up your cross and follow me'* (Matt. 16:24). But He did also promise that it would be the way of deep and lasting fulfilment and indescribable joy beginning now and lasting for ever. A difficult decision which hard way to take? Surely not! Dr Helen Roseveare writes, 'If

I truly believe in Him, I'll trust Him to desire for me that which is for my highest good, and to have planned for its fulfilment.'

Prayer: Heavenly Father, may we not resist you but as we hear your call on our lives, affections and wills, may we respond to you with glad and total surrender, for our good and for your glory. In Jesus' name. Amen

30 The sign of Jonah

Jesus loved the book of Jonah, and in the gospels we read that Jesus is *'One that is greater than Jonah'* (Luke 11:29-32 and Matt 12:39-41). Jesus, unlike Jonah, really died and did so, not for Himself or for His own sins, but willingly, for the sake of His enemies. Jesus freely went through awful God-forsakenness of the cross and the tomb, so that those who trust in Him would not have to experience the traumas of everlasting separation, but have everlasting life! (John 3:16) Jesus sank to the depths of judgment and turmoil so that we would not have to. He took the weight of God's wrath against sin on Himself, so that we who deserved nothing but being thrown overboard into Sheol, would be liberated from the idols of our hearts and set free to proclaim the forgiveness of Christ Jesus, and in His name love and serve the cities and nations of this needy world. Even as Jonah was a sign to the Ninevites, *said Jesus*, so also will the Son of Man be to this generation. *'The men of Nineveh will stand up at the judgment with this generation and condemn it, for they repented at the preaching of Jonah, and now one greater than Jonah is here.'*

For those who are united with Christ in faith, the unmistakable call of the Lord Jesus is to share His mission to, and compassion for, this fragile troubled world in our day and generation.

Prayer: Heavenly Father, thank you for Jesus. Thank you that He loved us and gave Himself up for us all. In His name and by His authority, infilled and empowered by the Holy Spirit, send us to live and speak the good news of the gospel, and as we hear your word to 'GO' may we respond with a wholehearted 'YES'. Amen

31 Postscript

Well then? *Is God vindictive, making His children do the things they don't want to do?* That's what Jonah thought: *'O Lord, is this not what I said when I was still at home?'* (4:2) and that's what I thought as well, until God, by His Holy Spirit, did a miracle of grace within my bigoted and stubborn heart. God doesn't want to make His disciples unhappy, but He does want to change us so that we are happy to do what He wants us to do! *'It is for freedom that Christ has set us free'!* (Gal. 5:1) As a young believer, I yearned to be *'Aglow with the Spirit and serve the Lord',* but in order for that to happen God had to discipline and sanctify me so that instead of bowing to the idols of my heart I was prepared to bow to Him. God is not vindictive – making us do what we least want to do – but rather He loves to change us so that we are happy to do what He wants us to do! He delights to transform us after the likeness of His obedient Son, so that by His grace, the only thing we yearn to do is to serve Him with all of our hearts! Having said 'Yes' to God and agreed to participate with Him through student work in the Republic of Ireland for three years, by the time I was eligible for a call to minister to a congregation some years later, the only place I wanted to serve God was the South of Ireland! For seventeen further years my beloved wife and partner in the gospel, Claire, and I set up home and raised our three children in the great city of Dublin. There we were privileged to experience the joy and blessing of ministering within the context of God's perfect will until God called us to a fresh challenge and new opportunity in Belfast.

And what of Jonah? Did he continue to think of God in hard and negative terms? Did he go on through life with a chip (and fish) on his shoulder or did he ever discover the delight of following the path of life and joy in the presence of the Lord? At the risk of tying up loose ends too tidily, how else would we have the story of Jonah before us unless it had been told by the prophet himself? And why would Jonah have shared his unflattering story if it hadn't been to say, 'I learned the hard way. Don't make these same mistakes yourself'! It's a great story. A great story about a great God's compassion for a great city, but most of all it's a great story because it points us to Jesus our Saviour.

'What I have vowed I will make good,' said Jonah, 'for *"Salvation comes from the Lord"*.'

Questions for personal or corporate study

JONAH CHAPTER 1

1. The Word of the Lord came to Jonah verse 1. In what ways have you experienced God communicating with you and how did you respond?

2. Jonah, like Adam and Eve before him (Gen. 3:8-10) tried to escape God's presence, but in what way is this impossible? (Ps. 139)

3. In running away from the Lord, Jonah 'went down' verses 3, 5 and 17, whereas God wants to raise him 'up'. Likewise the Prodigal Son (Luke 15:11-32) sank low before being being restored to fellowship with his loving Father. Discuss the path of repentance in the life of the believer.

4. These pagan sailors displayed more compass-ion than believing Jonah verses 13-14. Is that shocking especially in light of Jonah's testimony of verse 9?

5. In verse 3 we read 'But Jonah' and in verse 17 'But God'. What truth had Jonah forgotten? (1 Tim 2:4-6)

Bonus question: Since it is the Lord who has made the sea and land, verse 9, how ought those who profess faith in him care for rather than exploit the physical environment, as a Bible imperative? (Gen. 2:15)

JONAH CHAPTER 2

1. Having not prayed in Chapter 1:5-6, Jonah now prays! What brings about this change?

2. In contrast with some of the great prayers of the Bible e.g. Daniel 9, Isaiah 64, Jeremiah 32 and John 17, Jonah's prayer is self focussed, individualistic, naval gazing and not even using his own words! Before we criticise Jonah too harshly, how impoverished are our own prayers compared to these great texts?

3. Oddly while Jonah's prayers draw heavily upon the Psalms e.g. Psalms 3, 18 and 42, they contain no hint of sorrow for past disobedience nor repentance (cf the Ninevites

in Ch. 3:10). Does salvation verse 9 without repentance lead to joy in Christian service?

4. Jonah could clearly see the worthless idols verse 8 in the lives of the sailors and the Ninevites but had little ability to discern the idols of his own heart. Can we help each other identify those idolatrous things we love most and yet resist surrendering to the Lordship of Jesus within our specific contexts? (Phil. 2:5-11 and Col. 1:15-20)

JONAH CHAPTER 3

1. What was the Lord asking of Jonah on this second occasion? Ch 3:1 cf Ch 1:1. How had Jonah changed (or not)?

2. Both John the Baptist and Jesus (Matt. 3:2 and 4:17) called for repentance. Consider examples of such evidence in Nineveh and in your experience.(Joel 2:12-14 and Luke 19:1-9)

3. Jesus personally commends the Ninevites (Matt. 12:39-41) for their contriteness. (2 Chron. 7:14). What might Christian repentance practically look like within our culture for example in our attitudes to people of other races/religions/backgrounds?

JONAH CHAPTER 4

1. In Ch 3:10 God had compassion on the people of Nineveh. Jonah knew that this was

God's nature (Exod. 34:6-7). He had after all experienced it for himself in the belly of the fish but resented it when it was extended to those he did not like. Discuss!

2. Jonah had such a strong emotional reaction to what God did that he didn't like verse 1, he prayed again: this time asking to die verse 3 and verse 8. How does God seek to reorientate Jonah's negative way of thinking to help him see how God sees things? verses 6-11.

3. In what ways does Jonah's attitude grate with that of the Lord Jesus? (John 13:1-17, Mark 10:43-45, Rom. 5:6-8)

4. Compare God's nature in the book with that of Jonah the Prophet. Jonah was a believer but still needed to be made more like the Lord Jesus (Rom. 6, Gal. 5:22-26). Share how this life long process of sanctification can be encouraged in our lives.

5. In Matthew 16:4 Jesus says the only sign God will give unbelievers is the 'sign of Jonah'. What is this and for what reason? (Matt. 12:39-40)

Bonus question: Since studying the book of Jonah, what kind of person does God want me to become and what sort of thing does He now want me to do with gladness?